Bible Promises

Given to **Diane St. Martin**

On this **25th** day of **DECEMBER '91**

By **YOUR FRIENDS AT F.C.A.P.**

With this special message . . .

WITH LOVE + PRAYERS TO

"THANK YOU" FOR YOUR

FAITHFULNESS WITH OUR

FCAP GROUP.

PRECIOUS MOMENTS™

Bible Promises

SAM BUTCHER

THOMAS NELSON PUBLISHERS
Nashville

Published in Nashville, Tennessee, by Thomas Nelson, Inc.,
and distributed in Canada by Lawson Falle, Ltd.,
Cambridge, Ontario.

Printed in the United States of America.
ISBN: 0-8407-7457-5

Contents

Introduction 7

1. Promises of Blessings 9

2. Promises for Personal Needs 17

3. Promises for Relationships 33

Introduction

Even the most casual collector of Precious Moments℠ figurines senses the connection between the names of the figurines and verses in the Bible. This is no coincidence. Sam Butcher's faith has inspired the creation of the Precious Moments℠ illustrations.

Through the years Sam met many people who had problems in their lives and needed someone to tell them, "I'm here if you need me." Sam never liked to push people. So, instead, he made individual greeting cards. He found people really responded and would say, "If you would do greeting cards like these, so many people would be blessed."

This book is the first time Sam has shared the complete Bible verses that inspired the Precious Moments℠ art and figurines. He has divided the book into three sections: Promises of Blessings, Promises for Personal Needs, and Promises for Relationships. He shares these passages of Scripture with you so that you might be able to read them at times when you are having difficulty or needing an insight into your everyday life.

Promises of Blessings

Blessed Are the Peacemakers

Matthew 5:9: "Blessed are the peacemakers."

Blessed are the peacemakers,
For they shall be called sons of God.

Blessed are those who are persecuted for righteousness' sake,
For theirs is the kingdom of heaven. . . .

"Rejoice and be exceedingly glad, for great is your reward in heaven, for so they persecuted the prophets who were before you."

Matthew 5:9–10, 12

Make a Joyful Noise

Psalm 100:1: "Make a joyful shout to the Lord."

Make a joyful shout to the Lord, all you lands!
Serve the Lord with gladness;
Come before His presence with singing.

Know that the Lord, He is God;
It is He who has made us, and not
    we ourselves;
We are His people and the sheep of
    His pasture.

Enter into His gates with thanksgiving.
And into His courts with praise.
Be thankful to Him, and bless His name.
For the Lord is good;
His mercy is everlasting,
And His truth endures to all generations.

Psalm 100

To God Be the Glory

Psalm 29:2: "Praise the Lord's glorious name,"

Praise the Lord, you heavenly beings;
   praise His glory and power.

Praise the Lord's glorious name; bow down
   before the Holy One when He appears....

The Lord gives strength to His people and
   blesses them with peace.

Psalm 29:1–2, 11

Promises for Personal Needs

The Lord Is My Shepherd

Psalm 23:1: "The Lord is my shepherd."

The Lord is my shepherd;
I shall not want.
He makes me to lie down in green
  pastures;
He leads me beside the still waters.
He restores my soul;
He leads me in the paths of righteousness
For His name's sake.

Yea, though I walk through the valley of the
  shadow of death,
I will fear no evil;
For You are with me;
Your rod and Your staff, they comfort me.

You prepare a table before me in the
  presence of my enemies;
You anoint my head with oil;
My cup runs over.
Surely goodness and mercy shall follow me
All the days of my life;
And I will dwell in the house of the Lord
Forever.

Psalm 23

His Burden Is Light

*Matthew 11:30: "For My yoke is easy
and My burden is light."*

"Come to Me, all you who labor and are
heavy laden, and I will give you rest.

"Take My yoke upon you and learn from
Me, for I am gentle and lowly in heart,
and you will find rest for your souls.

"For My yoke is easy and *My burden
is light."*

Matthew 11:28–30

If God Be for Us,
Who Can Be Against Us?

Romans 8:31: "If God is for us, who can be against us?"

In view of all this, what can we say? If God
is for us, who can be against us? . . .

Who, then, can separate us from the love of
Christ?

Can trouble do it?

Or hardship or persecution or hunger or
poverty or danger or death?

For I am certain that nothing can separate
us from His love:

Neither the present nor the future,

Neither the world above nor the world
below.

Romans 8:31, 35, 38

Trust in the Lord

Psalm 37:3: "Trust in the Lord."

Trust in the Lord and do good;
Live in the land and be safe.
Seek your happiness in the Lord.
And He will give you your heart's desire.

Give yourself to the Lord.
Trust in Him, and He will help you.
He will make your righteousness shine
   like the noonday sun . . .

Soon the wicked will disappear;
You may look for them, but you won't
   find them.
But the humble will possess the land
And enjoy prosperity and peace.

Psalm 37:3–6, 10–12

Jesus Is the Light

John 8:12: "I am the light of the world."

Jesus spoke to the Pharisees again. *"I am the light of the world,"* He said. "Whoever follows Me will have the light of life and will never walk in darkness."

John 8:12

Onward Christian Soldiers

Ephesians 6:11: "Put on all the armor that
God gives you."

Put on all the armor that God gives you,
So that you will be able to stand up against
   the Devil's evil tricks. . . .

So stand ready,
With truth as a belt tight around your waist,
With righteousness as your breastplate,
And as your shoes the readiness to
   announce the Good News of peace.

At all times carry faith as a shield.
For with it you will be able to put out all
   the burning arrows shot by the Evil One.

And accept salvation as a helmet.
And the word of God as the sword which
   the Spirit gives you.

Do all this in prayer, asking for God's help.

Ephesians 6:11, 14–18

No Tears Past the Gate

I praise you, Lord, because you have saved
    me and kept my enemies from gloating
    over me.
I cried to you for help, O Lord my God,
    and you healed me; you kept me
    from the grave.
I was on my way to the depths below,
    but you restored my life.
Sing praise to the Lord,
    all his faithful people!
Remember what the Holy One has done,
    and give him thanks!
His anger lasts only a moment,
    his goodness for a lifetime.
Tears may flow in the night,
    but joy comes in the morning. . . .
Lord, you are my God;
    I will give you thanks forever.

Psalm 30:1–5; 11, 12

Promises for Relationships

Love Is Kind

I Corinthians 13:4:"Love suffers long and is kind."

Though I speak with the tongues of men and of angels but have not love, I have become as sounding brass or a clanging cymbal.

And though I have a gift of prophecy, and understand all mysteries and all knowledge, and though I have all faith, so that I could remove mountains, but have not love, I am nothing. . . .

Love suffers long and is kind; love does not envy; love does not parade itself, is not puffed up.

I Corinthians 13:1–4

Love Beareth All Things

I Corinthians 13:7 "Love bears all things."

Love does not behave rudely, does not seek its own, is not provoked, thinks no evil;

Does not rejoice in iniquity, but rejoices in the truth;

Love bears all things, believes all things, hopes all things, endures all things.

I Corinthians 13:5-7

Love One Another

John 15:12: "Love one another."

"My commandment is this: *love one another,* just as I love you.

"And you are My friends if you do what I command you. . . .

"You did not choose Me; I chose you and appointed you to go and bear much fruit, the kind of fruit that endures. And so the Father will give you whatever you ask of Him in My name.

"This, then, is what I command you: *love one another."*

John 15:12–14, 16–17

Bear One Another's Burdens

Galatians 6:2: "Help carry one another's burdens."

My brothers, if someone is caught in any kind of wrongdoing, those of you who are spiritual should set him right; but you must do it in a gentle way. . . .

Help carry one another's burdens, and in this way you will obey the law of Christ.

Galatians 6:1, 2

Let Not the Sun Go Down on Your Wrath

Ephesians 4:26: "Do not let the sun go down on your wrath."

This I say, therefore, and testify in the Lord, that you should no longer walk as the rest of the Gentiles walk. . . .

Therefore, putting away lying, each one speak truth with his neighbor, for we are members of one another.

"Be angry, and do not sin": *do not let the sun go down on your wrath,* nor give place to the devil.

Ephesians 4:17, 25–27

God Loveth a Cheerful Giver

2 Corinthians 9:7: "For God loves a cheerful giver."

But this I say: He who sows sparingly will also reap sparingly, and he who sows bountifully will also reap bountifully.

So let each one give as he purposed in his heart, not grudgingly or of necessity; *for God loves a cheerful giver.*

2 Corinthians 9:6–7

Love Never Fails

1 Corinthians 13: 8 "Love never fails."

Love never fails. But whether there are prophecies, they will fail; whether there are tongues, they will cease; whether there is knowledge, it will vanish away.

For we know in part and we prophesy in part.

But when that which is perfect has come, then that which is in part will be done away. . . .

And now abide faith, hope, love, these three; but the greatest of these is love.

1 Corinthians 13: 8–10, 13

REPORT CARD
Kindness .. A
Mercy .... A
Love .... A
faithfulness A

teacher